WELLINGTON

Prisoners in the dungeon

TESSA KRAILING

ILLUSTRATED BY
JON DAVIS

Nelson

The new words in this story are listed in the appropriate Word Wall Worksheet in the Teacher's Resource Pack for Level 4.

Thomas Nelson and Sons Ltd
Nelson House Mayfield Road
Walton-on-Thames Surrey
KT12 5PL UK

Thomas Nelson Australia
102 Dodds Street
South Melbourne
Victoria 3205 Australia

Nelson Canada
1120 Birchmount Road
Scarborough Ontario
M1K 5G4 Canada

Text © Tessa Krailing 1989
Illustrations © Thomas Nelson and Sons Ltd 1992
Illustrated by Jon Davis

First published by Macmillan Education Ltd 1989

This edition published by Thomas Nelson and Sons Ltd 1992

I(T)P   Thomas Nelson is an International
       Thomson Publishing Company

I(T)P   is used under licence

ISBN 0-17-422735-3
NPN 9 8 7 6

Printed in China

WELLINGTON SQUARE

Contents

Ghosts don't scare me

Mr Belter's class were going on a trip.
They were going to see a castle.
'Be quick!' said Mr Belter.
'Get into the bus.'
Rocky was very pleased about the trip.
'I've never been to a castle,' he said to Ben.
'Have you?'
'No,' said Ben. 'I've seen pictures but I
haven't been to one.'

The castle was a long way from
Waterloo School.
'Are we nearly there?' asked Kevin.
'Yes,' said Mr Belter.
'Just about another five minutes.'
The bus stopped outside the castle next
to the drawbridge.
The drawbridge went over a moat.
Rocky and the others jumped off the bus.
'Look at that moat,' said Rocky.
'It goes all the way around the castle!'
They had to go across the drawbridge to
get over the moat.
'Now keep together and follow me,'
said Mr Belter.

The children followed Mr Belter into
a big room.
'This is the Great Hall,' he said.
'It was built in 1241.'
Rocky and Ben looked around.
'Wow, this is big!' said Rocky.
'I think it's spooky,' said Ben.
'You are silly,' said Kevin.
'It isn't spooky.
It doesn't scare me!'
Rocky and Ben didn't believe Kevin.
They knew he was frightened in the
spooky Hall, just like they were.

Mr Belter took them to the Keep next.
They had to go up a lot of steps.
Kevin leaned over to look down but
Rocky and the others kept back.
'Be careful,' said Mr Belter to Kevin.
'Don't lean over too far.
You might fall!'
'I won't fall,' said Kevin.
'It doesn't scare me!'
'Come away from there!' shouted Mr Belter.
The others could see that Kevin was cross.

They left the Keep and went down lots
of steps.
'We are now in the dungeon,' said Mr Belter.
'What's a dungeon?' asked Jamila.
'A dungeon is where prisoners were kept,'
said Mr Belter.
'Sometimes they were kept without
food or water.
Some of the prisoners died and people
say there are ghosts here.'
'Ghosts!' said Ben.
'Ghosts don't scare me!' said Kevin.

Shut in the dungeon

The children were pleased when Mr Belter
said it was time to go.
They followed him quickly but
Kevin was still looking around.
Suddenly the door of the dungeon
slammed shut!
Kevin ran over to the door but
he couldn't open it.
He was left inside all on his own.
'Hey!' shouted Kevin.
'Let me out!
I can't open the door!'
Kevin began to bang on the door.
He looked through the bars in the door but
there was no-one there.

Kevin looked around the dungeon.
It was cold and frightening.
Kevin jumped.
What was that?
He could hear strange noises.
Were there rats in the dungeon or
was it a ghost?
'I'm not frightened,' said Kevin out loud.
But he WAS frightened!
He wanted to get out of the dungeon and
find the others.
'Let me out! Let me out!' he shouted as
he banged on the door.
But no-one came.
Kevin sat down.
He was cold, unhappy and frightened.

Mr Belter and the others went outside the
castle and onto the grass.
'Time for something to eat,' said Mr Belter.
They all sat down and soon everyone
was eating.
Rocky suddenly looked around.
'Where's Kevin?' he asked.
'Isn't he here?' said Ben.
'I can't see him,' said Rocky.
'We'd better tell Mr Belter.'
Rocky and Ben told Mr Belter that
they couldn't see Kevin.

Mr Belter looked around.
'No, I can't see him,' he said.
'We'd better go and look for him.
Tessa and Tony, you look in the Great Hall.
I'll go up to the Keep.

Rocky and Ben, you go down to the dungeon and
see if Kevin is there.
You others get on with your food.
If Kevin comes back tell him to wait here.
We won't be long.'

TO THE
CASTLE

Rocky and Ben made their way back to
the dungeon.
They looked through the bars in the door and
saw Kevin inside the dungeon.
'There he is!' said Ben.
'He can't get out,' said Rocky.
'Don't let him see us,' said Ben.
'Then we can scare him!'
'How can we do that?' asked Rocky.
Ben looked around.
He saw some old, rusty chains.
'Look at those chains,' he said.
'We could make a frightening noise with them.'

Rocky and Ben picked up the chains and
rattled them.
Kevin jumped up.
What was that noise?
It sounded like chains rattling!
Kevin knew that ghosts rattled chains!
He ran to the door.
'Let me out!' he shouted.

Rocky and Ben opened the door slowly.

Kevin jumped back.

By this time he was very frightened.

'Boo!' shouted Ben as he ran into the dungeon.

Rocky followed him.

Kevin looked so frightened they both laughed.

'We were the ghosts,' they said.

'I knew that all the time,' said Kevin.

'You didn't scare me!'

Rocky and Ben laughed again.

'Yes we did,' said Rocky.

'You should have seen the look on your face!'

Prisoners

Kevin was cross.
He went over to the door.
Rocky and Ben were laughing so much they
didn't see what he was doing.
Kevin left the dungeon quickly and
slammed the door behind him.
Rocky and Ben were shut in the dungeon!
They were prisoners!
'You see what it's like shut in a dungeon!'
said Kevin.

Rocky and Ben stopped laughing.
'Come on, Kevin, let us out,' shouted Ben.
But Kevin wasn't there.
The boys banged on the door and
shouted but no-one came.
'We shouldn't have frightened him with
those chains,' said Rocky.
'No,' said Ben. 'And we shouldn't have
laughed at him.'
'We're prisoners now,' said Rocky.
'What are we going to do?'
'Kevin will come back,' said Ben.
'Or Mr Belter will come looking for us.'
'Yes,' said Rocky.
'But how long will we be here?
I don't like it.
It's cold and there are strange noises.'
'Let's bang on the door again,' said Ben.
'Someone will hear us.'

Mr Belter came back from the Keep.
He saw Kevin with the others.
'Where have you been?' he asked.
'Just looking around,' said Kevin.
'Well, it's time to go.
You've kept us all waiting,' said Mr Belter.
He told the children to pick up the rubbish and
make their way back to the bus.

Mr Belter made sure there was no rubbish
left on the grass and then he followed
the children.
'Get in,' he said.
He watched them get into the bus.
'Where are Rocky and Ben?' he asked.
'Oh, they were in the Great Hall when
I last saw them,' said Kevin.
Mr Belter was cross.
'Now I will have to go and find them,'
he said.

Rocky and Ben looked through the bars in
the door.
'There's no-one there,' said Ben.
Rocky jumped as a rat ran across the dungeon.
'We've got to get out of here!' he said.
'I don't like rats and I don't like ghosts!'
'There are no ghosts,' said Ben.
'WE were the ghosts, remember.
WE rattled the chains.'
'What's that noise, then?' asked Rocky.
'That wasn't a rat!'
Ben looked through the bars.
'Someone will come soon,' he said.
But no-one came.

Soon it was getting dark.

The castle was empty.

Mr Belter went back to the bus.

'They weren't in the Great Hall,' he told the children.

'Are you sure you saw them there?' he asked Kevin.

'Yes, Mr Belter,' said Kevin, not looking at the teacher.

'Well, I had better go and find the caretaker,' said Mr Belter.

Where are Rocky and Ben?

Mr Belter left the children on the bus and
went to find the caretaker.
'Two of the boys are missing,' he told
the caretaker.
'Could you come and look for them with me?'
The caretaker said he would look for the
boys with Mr Belter.
'I've looked in the Great Hall,' said
Mr Belter as they left the caretaker's room.

'Let's go to the Keep,' said the caretaker.
'They might be up there.'
Mr Belter and the caretaker went up the
steps to the Keep.
They had to go carefully as it was
getting dark.
'Rocky! Ben!' shouted Mr Belter.
'Are you there?'
But Rocky and Ben were not in the Keep.
They were prisoners in the dungeon!

Mr Belter and the caretaker looked around
the castle.
'I'm going back to talk to the children,'
said Mr Belter.
He went back to the bus.
'I think you know where Rocky and
Ben are,' he said to Kevin.
'Now you had better tell me quickly.
It's getting very dark and we have to
find them.'

Kevin was very frightened now because
Mr Belter looked so cross.
'They are in the dungeon,' he said.
'I got left behind and when they found me
they frightened me by rattling
some chains.
I was cross so I shut them in.'
Mr Belter was not pleased.
'That was a silly thing to do,' he said.
'But Rocky and Ben were silly too.
You come with me, Kevin, and we'll let
them out.'

Mr Belter told Kevin to get off the bus and
follow him.
Kevin didn't want to go back to the
dungeon but he did as he was told.
Mr Belter saw the caretaker coming across
the drawbridge.
He told him the boys were in the dungeon.
'That was a silly thing to do,'
the caretaker told Kevin.
Kevin didn't say anything at all.

They went down the dark steps to the dungeon.
The caretaker opened the door.
Rocky and Ben were very pleased to see
Mr Belter but they were not too pleased
to see Kevin.
'He slammed the door and made us prisoners,'
said Rocky.
'I know,' said Mr Belter.
'Kevin was silly, but you did a silly thing
as well, rattling the chains!'

'Who is rattling the chains now?'
asked Ben.
'Who is outside the door?' asked Rocky.
'No-one!' said the caretaker.
The chains rattled again.
'I think we had better get out of here!'
said Mr Belter.
And they all left the dark dungeon very quickly!